D1324486

THE QUEEN
AND
PRINCESS ANNE

Lisa Sheridan

PHOTOGRAPHS BY
STUDIO LISA

PUBLISHED BY AUTHORITY OF
HER MAJESTY THE QUEEN

John Murray
FIFTY ALBEMARLE STREET LONDON

BY APPOINTMENT PHOTOGRAPHERS TO
H. M. QUEEN ELIZABETH THE QUEEN MOTHER

STUDIO LISA LTD

© Lisa Sheridan 1959

*Printed in Great Britain by Hazell Watson & Viney, Ltd., London & Aylesbury,
and published by John Murray (Publishers) Ltd.*

Introduction

THE photographs in this book of the Queen with Princess Anne were taken at Windsor Castle one lovely summer's day of 1959, immediately prior to the Canadian Tour. Then, while her mother was away from home, Princess Anne was enrolled as a Brownie. She was not able to wear a Brownie uniform, which had been waiting for her before the Queen went away. But, when the Queen came home again at the beginning of August, the Princess had completed her first term as a Brownie and was able to show her mother the photographs of herself and her Brownie companions taken in the gardens of Buckingham Palace. These were taken at the last meeting of that first session before the Pack disbanded for the holidays.

Holiday times bring the Prince of Wales home. Brother and sister are good friends and have many interests in common. At Buckingham Palace they have a pair of love-birds as pets. The Princess tells me that they are called Annie and Davy and that they are red, blue and green. Pets play an important part in the lives of the Royal children. At Windsor Castle Princess Anne has her pony, Greensleeves. Greensleeves often goes on holiday with the Princess. She has travelled to Balmoral with the family this year. The corgi dogs (particularly the "nursery corgis," Whisky and Sherry) trot around with the Princess from room to room, and often romp with her in the garden. Princess Anne spends much time caring for her pets and has the same sympathetic understanding of them which her mother already showed when quite a child herself.

In the Palace schoolroom, at Buckingham Palace, the Princess shares her lessons with two other little girls. You will see a photograph of the three of them together in this book. Princess Anne is learning to play the piano which she enjoys, but she specially likes history lessons for she is learning about the interesting reign of Queen Elizabeth I. History must be a particularly fascinating subject to a little girl who lives so frequently in the houses where so many Kings and Queens of our history books have actually lived themselves. At Windsor Castle,

3

where the Princess often spends the weekends, she is reminded that Elizabeth the First once lived there herself and rode through the park and around the great building as merrily as she is doing today. There our Princess plays in the same corridors, peeps into the great halls and, though inevitably time has brought some change, she knows that those stones of Windsor Castle could tell many a story which has now been lost to history. It is not surprising that Princess Anne finds history an enthralling study. Even when she rides to Frogmore Gardens, in that place of peace and natural beauty, she sees the Royal Mausoleum where Queen Victoria and the Prince Consort are buried.

Frogmore Gardens lie close to the Castle and on the lake there the Royal Family often use the little blue sailing dinghy during the weekends. There are a number of photographs in this book taken in the gardens when the Queen and Princess Anne were using the dinghy, or resting after a ride.

Royal Lodge, the country home of Queen Elizabeth the Queen Mother, lies on the Royal Estate at Windsor, not far from the Castle. This offers an easy comradeship between the older and the younger members of the Royal Family who visit each other's homes frequently. Now that both Prince Charles and Princess Anne have been taught to swim by Prince Philip, the swimming-pool at Royal Lodge is a favourite resort in the summer months.

In my photograph on page 21 it is particularly interesting to see Princess Anne's straight back. Her parents place emphasis on physical development and the taut little body is doubtless due to the various healthful recreations in which the child is encouraged. There is the weekly dancing class at the Palace; there is riding at weekends in Windsor, and many a quick spin on her green bicycle round the garden-paths of Buckingham Palace. Then, in summer and winter alike there is swimming, for the swimming-pool at Buckingham Palace can be heated when necessary. Prince Philip teaches her to play tennis correctly. The Princess also attends a gym class once a week and now the Brownies are beginning a variety of physical exercises. This very lively little girl enters into all such activities with her customary vitality and enthusiasm.

The Queen and Prince Philip are devoted to an ideal of family life and have as closely-knit a united life with their children as one may find in any family in the land. They wish their children to grow up as naturally as possible without undue evidence of their important status. This educational policy is being most successfully developed as those who have had the privilege of meeting the Royal children in their home life always testify.

Some years ago when I photographed the Queen and Princess

Margaret as children I was impressed by the informality of their home lives and by their unaffected charm. When asked, as I often was asked, "What are the Princesses really like at home?" I always felt I should reply: "Really natural children. Children privileged by a sense of security in knowing themselves each a treasured part in an affectionate united family."

Certainly the same words would serve today in describing the home life of our present Royal Family where Princess Anne is growing up and is now nine years old.

LISA SHERIDAN

THE QUEEN AND PRINCESS ANNE

In the grounds of Windsor Castle a few steps lead through a covered passage from the East Terrace to a secluded garden on the south side. As the Queen and Princess Anne pause for a moment, Sugar promptly curls up for one of the brief naps she likes so much.

The grey stone-work of Windsor Castle makes a delightful setting for the flowers which grow against the ancient walls of the castle. Here a profusely flowering red rose-tree has caught Princess Anne's attention.

There is a happy informality between Princess Anne and her mother, and they always enjoy each other's company. It is interesting to see that the Princess has already reached the height of her mother's shoulder.

When this photograph was taken Princess Anne was nearly nine years old. She has paused for a moment in the garden at Windsor Castle where red and yellow roses climb the great walls. She is looking forward to a ride on her pony which is in the paddock close-by.

When the Queen and Prince Philip are in London, they go with their children to Windsor Castle for the weekend. There the Queen and her family have the pleasures and the informality of a country home. Riding is of course a special enjoyment on these occasions.

The Princess is encouraged to care for and unharness her pony herself; this she loves doing. In the paddock close to Windsor Castle she is seen with Greensleeves. William, standing by the Queen, is the Welsh pony on which the Royal children learnt to ride.

Greensleeves is now Princess Anne's pony. She is a Welsh-bred strawberry roan and was bought six years ago for Prince Charles when Princess Anne was only just starting to ride.

(*Above*) Princess Anne is starting for a ride from the George IV Gate on the South Front of Windsor Castle to Frogmore Gardens (*below*).

Cascades of blue wistaria make a lovely background for the young
Princess after a canter from Windsor Castle to Frogmore Gardens.

The Queen watches her daughter canter across the grass. At the first indication of leisure moments, Sugar flops down as close as possible to her mistress. Though apparently lost to the world, the corgi is fully awake at the least sign of the Queen's intention to get up. In a flash she is ready to trot to the next halting-place and the next "forty winks".

Greensleeves looks much nicer when the ears are pricked forward.
Princess Anne tried to make her do so for the photograph, but the pony
preferred not to bother.

A rest in Frogmore Gardens by the summer-house which is usually called "The Ruin" as it was built as a sham ruin during the period when such garden ornaments were fashionable. The Queen, as Princess Elizabeth, and Princess Margaret used to meet here as Guides and Sea Rangers during the war.

Boating on the lake in Frogmore Gardens. The Queen is offering some advice, but Princess Anne likes doing the actual work herself.

Prince Charles and Princess Anne are never allowed to go out in the boat alone. Princess Anne is taking off the tarpaulin from the boat to make it ready for use with her mother. Her attention has been caught by the antics of the moorhens who skim across the water.

Whisky tries to help but the Princess has thrown him a stick so that she can get on with the job.

Back in the garden in the grounds of Windsor Castle with the Queen's corgi, Sugar, who closes her eyes in sentimental rapture at the prospect of another "forty winks."

Princess Anne with Sugar. The dogs are inseparable from the Royal children and always go with them for weekends, or when the family is visiting Sandringham or Balmoral Castle. Princess Anne loves looking after the dogs herself.

Sugar is the Queen's dog. She is the mother of Whisky and Sherry who are called the "nursery dogs." Whisky belongs to Prince Charles and Sherry to Princess Anne.

Another day is nearly over. Sugar takes the opportunity to snatch a few dreams in uninterrupted comfort.

A few days later Princess Anne was enrolled as a Brownie. Here she is waiting to attend one of the meetings which take place in the gardens of Buckingham Palace.

After making their Promise at the opening of the meeting, the
Brownies settle down to get instructions about the jobs in hand.

The Brownie Pack divides into groups of six and report to the Brown Owl.

The First Buckingham Palace Brownie Pack, to which Princess Margaret used to belong, meet, and keep their equipment, in the gardens of the Palace. The Pack, of 24 members, meets in term-time every week for an hour after school.

The two Brownies with Princess Anne are her schoolroom friends, Susan Babington-Smith (on her right) and Caroline Hamilton, with whom she does lessons in the Palace.

Going home after the Brownie meeting.